Endpapers:
Relief from Temple of the Sun at Konarak,
photograph by Carol Guyer

THE
ART
OF
INDIA

by Shirley Glubok

Designed by Gerard Nook

Special Photography by
Alfred H. Tamarin and Carol Guyer

THE MACMILLAN COMPANY
Collier-Macmillan Limited, London

Bronze Parvati, The Metropolitan Museum of Art,
bequest of Cora Timken Burnett, 1957

The author gratefully acknowledges the assistance of:
ASCHWIN LIPPE, Former Associate Curator of Far Eastern Art, The Metropolitan Museum of Art
ANAND KRISHNA, Deputy Director, Bharat Kala Bhavan, Banaras, Hindu University
PRUDENCE HARPER, Associate Curator of Ancient Near Eastern Art, The Metropolitan Museum of Art
LOIS KATZ, Associate Curator in Charge of Oriental Art, The Brooklyn Museum
ISABEL WELLISZ
PETER POPE

Other books by Shirley Glubok:
THE ART OF ANCIENT EGYPT
THE ART OF LANDS IN THE BIBLE
THE ART OF ANCIENT GREECE
THE ART OF THE NORTH AMERICAN INDIAN
THE ART OF THE ESKIMO
THE ART OF ANCIENT ROME
THE ART OF AFRICA
ART AND ARCHAEOLOGY
THE ART OF ANCIENT PERU
THE ART OF THE ETRUSCANS
THE ART OF ANCIENT MEXICO
KNIGHTS IN ARMOR
THE FALL OF THE AZTECS
THE FALL OF THE INCAS
DISCOVERING TUT-ANKH-AMEN'S TOMB
DISCOVERING THE ROYAL TOMBS AT UR
HOME AND CHILD LIFE IN COLONIAL DAYS

Cover illustrations: Rajput miniatures, The Metropolitan Museum of Art.
Front: Krishna overcoming Kaliya (detail), Rogers Fund, 1927.
Back: Raga (musical mode), Rogers Fund, 1918. Photographs by Alfred H. Tamarin

India is a country in Asia, so huge that it is called a subcontinent. The Himalayas, the highest mountains in the world, form the northern boundary of India and separate it from the rest of Asia. The entire country is a peninsula that juts southward into the Indian Ocean.

India is a land of opposites with rich river valleys and barren wastelands, fertile plains and arid deserts. There are also dense forests and tropical jungles.

The history of India stretches back about five thousand years. Through all of these years the hundreds of millions of people living there have worshiped their gods in different ways.

Three of the world's great religions, Buddhism, Hinduism and Jainism, started in India. Followers of these religions built magnificent temples, and decorated them with sculpture and paintings. Almost all art in India is religious.

The earliest civilization in India arose about 2500 B.C. in the fertile valley of the Indus River.

Miniature reversed

Miniature from the Ratan Sas (detail),
Museum of Fine Arts, Boston

3

The ancient Indus Valley people built great cities. Harappa and Mohenjo-Daro were the two most important. The palaces, workshops, granaries, assembly halls, drainage systems and public baths in these cities reveal a highly developed civilization.

This small bronze statuette of a girl, only four and a half inches high, is from Mohenjo-Daro. She is dancing with her hand on her hip and bangle bracelets on her arm.

Important people had little stone stamp seals with pictures carved into them to mark things with their own sign. The stamp seal was pressed onto wet clay, leaving an impression with a raised design. Thus an object could be stamped with the mark of the owner of the seal.

National Museum, New Delhi,
photograph Archaeological Survey of India

Below are two impressions made from stamp seals, one showing a rhinoceros and the other an elephant. These seals, less than two and a half inches square, could be worn on a cord passed through a loop in the back. Today no one is able to read the ancient writing on the seals.

The Indus Valley civilization lasted about a thousand years, then came to a sudden end. The land was conquered by invaders from the north.

Most of the Indus River Valley lies within the borders of West Pakistan.

National Museum, New Delhi

A famous ruler of India was the Emperor Asoka, born about 300 B.C. Asoka set up tall stone pillars throughout his empire, with figures of animals on the capitals, or tops. One of the capitals, at left, with four lions seated back to back, has become the national emblem of India. The column was erected in honor of Buddha who was the founder of Buddhism, one of the great religions of India, which later spread to China and Japan.

At right is a stone head of Buddha, in deep thought, meditating. The name Buddha means the Enlightened One, "he who knows all things." Buddha's real name was Prince Siddhartha.

National Museum, New Delhi,
photograph Archaeological Survey of India

From Ratnagiri,
photograph Archaeological
Survey of India

Buddha grew up in a palace, protected from misery and pain. Then suddenly, all in one day, he came upon a suffering man, a sick man and a dead man. The prince decided to give up his life of luxury and devote himself to helping other people. He spent years wandering through India praying, fasting and teaching. At left is a standing stone Buddha.

The Buddha at right is seated on a lotus flower. This beautiful flower, which rises from the dirt and mud at the bottom of a pond, became the symbol of the beauty of Buddha's teachings, which rise above unhappiness and misery in the world. Buddha sits with his legs crossed. His hands are in a position which shows that he is teaching. He is surrounded by Bodhisattvas, beings of complete enlightenment, who dedicated themselves to relieving the misery of the world.

India Museum, Calcutta,
photograph Archaeological Survey of India

Government of India Tourist Office

At left is the Great Stupa at Sanchi in Central India. A stupa is a large mound of earth, bricks or stone, symbolizing the dome of heaven on top of the world. Relics of the Buddha, objects connected with him and his followers, were buried underneath. The Great Stupa is about two thousand years old.

A stone railing surrounds it, with four gateways, at the four points of the compass. Worshipers walk around the stupa mound inside the railing to pray or meditate.

At right is a close-up view of the eastern gateway, carved with scenes showing events in Buddha's various lives. It is believed in India that when a person dies his soul lives on and is reborn in another form. This is called reincarnation. The Buddha is said to have lived in various forms before he was born a prince.

Many elephants are carved on the gateway. Elephants are considered symbols of power and authority. The graceful female figure in the lower right corner is a tree spirit called a *yakshi*.

Photograph by
Eliot Elisofon

India is famous for its man-made caves, hollowed out of the solid living rock of steep cliffs. The caves served as worshiping halls and as quarters for monks. To dig out the caves, thousands of tons of rock had to be cut away and hauled off. Wooden bolts were inserted in holes cut into the rock. When soaked with water, the wood expanded, breaking off huge blocks of stone. At right is a view of the Ajanta caves near Aurangabad in East Central India. Every one of the openings in the cliff is the entrance to a separate Buddhist cave temple.

Another group of caves was made at Ellora, about fifty miles from Ajanta. In the midst of the caves, a spectacular temple, Kailasanatha, was carved out of the rocky mountainside, like a giant piece of sculpture. Kailasanatha is dedicated to Siva, one of the three principal forms of god in the Hindu religion.

Photograph by Carol Guyer

At left is a view of the interior of one of the Ajanta caves. The carved walls and pillars of this Buddhist worshiping hall are cut out of the living rock. In the center of the cave, also cut out of the rock, is a domed form in the shape of a stupa with a large Buddha seated on a throne.

The figure above, painted on a wall in another of the Ajanta caves, represents a Bodhisattva wearing a high crown with sapphires to symbolize his royal birth. This is one of the few cave paintings that have survived.

To paint a wall its surface was first smoothed, then coated with plaster and carefully polished with an elephant's tusk. Then it was covered with whitewash. The artist made a black and white sketch and went over it with red ochre. Colors were ground from minerals and plants, then mixed with a gummy substance to make them stick to the wall.

Photograph by
Eliot Elisofon

The Shore Temple at Mamallapuram, a seaport near the southern tip of India, was constructed to honor the Hindu god Siva. This temple has been standing at the edge of the sea for more than a thousand years.

Near the Shore Temple stands a huge cliff about eighty feet long, carved with figures in full life size. At left is a part of the cliff covered with carvings which represent the legend of the descent of the Holy River Ganges from the northern Himalayas into India. In this relief the creatures of the earth are giving thanks to the gods for the great Ganges River.

Photograph by Carol Guyer

In the Hindu religion God has three forms, each with a different name: Brahma, the creator; Siva, the destroyer; and Vishnu, the preserver.

Brahma, above, has four faces to represent the four points of the compass. They show that he is present everywhere in the universe. Brahma's goose, on which he rides, sits at his feet. Three of Brahma's hands hold objects closely associated with him: a rosary, or string of prayer beads, a ladle and a water bottle. The open palm of the lower left hand shows that he is granting a favor.

Below, Vishnu, the preserver, is stretched out on the coils of the serpent giant Ananta. When Vishnu sleeps on Ananta, who never dies, the strength of all creation is eternally renewed. Vishnu's gentle smile shows his deep love for all living creatures.

When a god was needed on earth, he appeared in many forms, or incarnations. Vishnu came to earth in ten incarnations. Among them were a fish, a tortoise, a boar, a lion, as well as Krishna and Rama, who became heroes of many popular legends.

Prince of Wales Museum, Bombay

Hindu temples were often clustered together in temple cities. At left is a view of a cluster of temples at Bhuvanesvar, in Orissa, in Eastern India. The great temple, called the Lingaraja, has a tall tower rising over the most sacred area. Animal figures and small models of the tower itself decorate the surface.

The pillared porch, which leads to the holiest part of the temple, is lower than the tower and to the left of it. A sacred dancing hall is also part of the temple. Other shrines, part of the temple complex, are in the foreground.

The carving at right is on one of the temples in the Bhuvanesvar group. The tall figure is a Hindu god, towering over a smaller human form. It is said that in ancient times there were about seven hundred temples in Bhuvanesvar. Today only about one hundred remain.

The Temple of the Sun, built near the sea at Konarak in Orissa, is about seven hundred years old. Its main tower, nearly two hundred feet high, has fallen into ruins. Piles of sculpture and rock are all that remain of the tower.

Only the porch of the temple has survived, as shown at right, below. The porch is in the form of a giant chariot in which Surya, the Hindu sun god, rides across the heavens. The building seems to rest on twelve large chariot wheels carved at its base. Colossal stone horses draw the heavenly chariot.

Above, at right, is a close-up of one of the wheels. It is covered with carved decoration.

The whole building is alive with sculptured forms. Statues of heavenly musicians stand on the roof of the temple. The musician at left, beating a drum, is large enough to be seen from a great distance.

These figures are carved on marble temples in the sacred city of Mt. Abu, in Rajasthan, in Northwestern India. The city was built to honor the gods of Jainism, one of India's living religions.

The Jaina religion was founded by a man named Mahavira, who lived around the time of Buddha. Jainism teaches extreme gentleness toward all living things. No creature large or small may be harmed.

It is said that gods came to Mt. Abu to visit the earth and mingle freely with people.

Beautiful white marble was found near the mountains. It was quarried on the plain below the mountain and dragged four thousand feet to the top. Every space in the temples, both inside and out, was decorated.

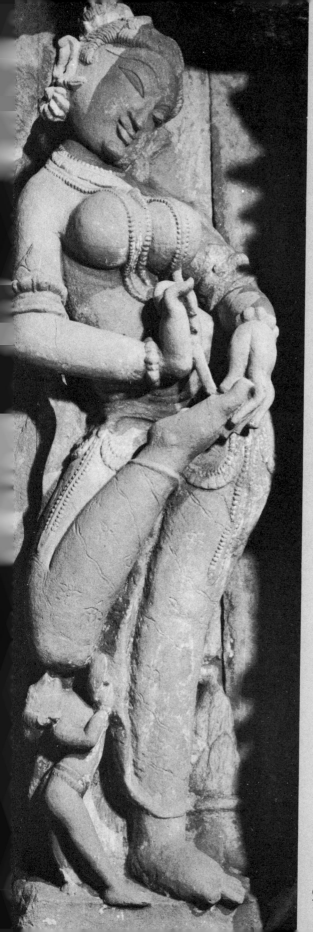

Photograph by Carol Guyer

Some of the temples in the large group at Khajuraho, in Central India, are Jaina. The temples are covered with carvings representing gods, goddesses and other heavenly creatures, as well as human beings and animals.

The figures on the Khajuraho temples are remarkable for their beauty and feeling of movement. Some of the bodies have unnaturally long, slim legs and blown-up proportions. And often they are shown in almost impossible positions. Yet they are so full of life and action that they seem natural. At left is a girl removing a thorn from her foot, with the help of a dwarf. At right is a wall carving on one of the Jaina temples at Khajuraho. The little figure at the top, seated cross-legged, represents a supernatural being called a Jaina. Below him are larger figures of his father and mother, who are still mortals.

Government of India
Tourist Office

At the temple of Srirangam, near Trichinopoly, in Southern India, an entire row of columns was carved into statues of prancing horses with riders. Figures representing warriors support the forelegs of the rearing horses.

In very ancient times in India animals were worshiped as gods. The bull came to be associated with the Hindu god Siva, and a bull named Nandi served as Siva's mount, the animal on which he rode. Nandi himself was worshiped as a god. There is a popular belief that if a woman touches a statue of Nandi it will help her to have children. Below is a stone Nandi from Southern India.

Avery Brundage Collection,
M. H. de Young Memorial
Museum, San Francisco,
photograph by Alfred H. Tamarin

Photograph by
Martin Hürlimann

30

Ganesa, a cheerful, chubby creature with an elephant head and human body, is perhaps the most beloved of the Hindu gods. The son of Siva, he is known as Lord of Obstacles—he who clears the way.

The Ganesa at left, from Mysore, in Southern India, was carved of a fine-grained stone known as chloritic schist. The stone is soft when taken from the ground and can be cut with sharp detail. Then, when exposed to the air, it becomes hard.

The temples in Halebid and Belur, in Mysore, are richly decorated with images carved in chloritic schist. The figure at right is dancing with a tiny orchestra at her feet.

Government of India
Tourist Office

Hindu religious images made of bronze were sometimes carried out of the temples for processions and festivals. The images were dressed in clothes and decked in jewels.

The gods most often represented were Siva and Vishnu and their consorts or wives. At left, Siva, as Nataraja, Lord of the Dance, dances on the body of the demon dwarf of ignorance. With his four arms in motion, Siva is demonstrating the continuing cycle of life— creation, preservation and destruction. His hands hold a small drum to represent the vibrations of the first sound of creation, and a tongue from the flame of destruction. One hand is raised in a gesture of protection; the other points to his uplifted foot, signifying salvation.

At right, Vishnu, the preserver of the world, is represented as Narasimha, half man half lion.

Nelson Gallery—Atkins Museum

33

Musée Gimet,
photograph by
Alfred H. Tamarin

Tanjore Art Gallery,
photograph Archaeological
Survey of India

Krishna, another of the earthly forms of the Hindu god Vishnu, was the hero of many youthful adventures. These two bronzes show him as a child. Krishna was a merry, mischievous lad who played pranks on the milkmaids. He would upset their pails of milk and run off with their freshly churned butter.

At right is another bronze statue of the god Siva Nataraja. He is performing inside a ring of fire which stands for the whole of the universe to which he gives life and movement.

The Detroit Institute of Arts

Parvati, the wife of Siva, is shown as a beautiful, gracious woman with long, slender arms and legs, a slim waist and full breasts. She represents the ideal of Indian beauty, which was handed down from one generation of artists to the next. There were rules which gave the artist the exact measurements to use.

At right is a female saint of Siva who punished herself in her worship of him. She inflicted great suffering on herself and refused food. Siva rewarded her by permitting her to accompany his dance by playing cymbals.

Freer Gallery of Art,
photograph by Alfred H. Tamarin

These figures are hollow bronze statues made, or cast, by the lost wax method. In this method a clay core is covered with a layer of wax, which is carefully modeled to the exact form of the final image. An outer coating of clay is added, in which small openings are left at the top and bottom. Heat is applied, making the wax melt and flow out. A hollow space is left inside, into which hot liquid bronze is poured. When cool, the clay cover and the inner core are removed. The bronze figure was worked with a chisel to give it a fine finish.

Nelson Gallery—Atkins Museum

In Rajasthan, in Northwestern India, Hindu princes had their books of history, legends and poetry illustrated with small, finely drawn paintings called miniatures. Adventures from the life of Krishna were a favorite theme.

Throughout his youth Krishna fought demons sent to kill him by his uncle, the wicked King Kamsa. One demon was a forest fire which threatened to destroy Krishna and his companions and their cows. In the miniature at right, Krishna is in a tree swallowing flames. His friends, the milkmaids, cover their eyes so they will not be blinded by the miracle.

Prince of Wales Museum, Bombay

Another time the king sent the serpent demon Aghasur to swallow Krishna and his friends. Krishna swelled up so much that he burst from the head of the demon and saved himself and his friends. This painting illustrates both events. The two trees in the center divide the scene.

Krishna's love for the beautiful milkmaid Radha is told and retold in countless Hindu songs and stories. In the illustration at right Krishna and Radha are together in the forest.

Krishna's adventures are also the subject of the Mahabharata, an epic or long narrative poem about the struggle between gods and heros that has been a favorite of Indian people for hundreds of years.

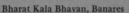
Bharat Kala Bhavan, Banares

The Cleveland Museum of Art,
Mr. and Mrs. William H. Marlatt Fund

The story of the goddess Durga, a beautiful woman with ten arms who rides a tiger, is illustrated in this miniature painting from the Punjab Hills at the foot of the Himalayas.

A bull demon, Mahisa, had driven the gods out of their heavenly kingdom. To defeat the demon, the gods gave Durga divine weapons for each of her ten hands. When the bull demon saw Durga coming to attack him, he tried to capture her by assuming many fierce disguises. Finally, Durga killed him with a spear.

Rajput miniature paintings are boldly drawn and daring in color.

Prince Rama, another earthly form of the Hindu god Vishnu, is the hero of the epic, the Ramayana. According to the story, a wicked king named Ravana, with ten heads and twenty arms, kidnaped Rama's beautiful wife, Sita, and carried her off in his winged chariot. Jatayu, king of the vultures, tried to rescue Sita, but Ravana wounded him with a hail of arrows. Luckily the dying bird lived long enough to tell Rama about the kidnaping of his wife.

Rama obtained the help of Sugriva, king of the monkeys. Sugriva called up an army of millions of monkeys and bears, led by the great ape Hanuman, son of the wind god.

King Ravana lived in a golden palace on the island of Lanka, which is the old name for Ceylon. To reach Lanka, the monkeys built a great shining bridge of rocks and trees and crossed over to fight King Ravana and his men. Finally Prince Rama vanquished the ten-headed king in single combat and rescued Sita.

Bharat Kala Bhavan, Banares

Bharat Kala Bhavan, Banares

The Metropolitan Museum of Art,
Rogers Fund, 1955,
photograph by Alfred H. Tamarin

Shortly after Rama's marriage to Sita, Rama's father, King Dasaratha, decided to give up his throne to his son. But Rama's stepmother cheated him out of the throne and he was sent to live in the forest. Laksmana, his brother, and Sita went with him. At left, they are in the forest dressed in garments of leaves.

Events in the life of Mahavira, the founder of Jainism, were favorite subject for Jaina manuscripts. This miniature represents Mahavira renouncing his earthly life. He is plucking out his hair before Shakra, king of the gods. Mahavira is exchanging his worldly clothing for monk's attire. The triangles at the bottom show that the scene occurred in the mountains.

Early Buddhist manuscripts were written on long, narrow palm leaves held together with string. At right is a painting of a goddess from an old Buddhist book.

The Metropolitan Museum of Art,
purchase, 1955,
photograph by Alfred H. Tamarin

The civilization of India, one of the oldest in the world, is very different from those of Europe and America. The art of India—with its monumental shrines and temples, sculptured figures of gods and goddesses, and colorful miniatures telling stories of lengendary heroes—helps us to understand the long history of this fascinating land, as well as how millions of Indians think and live and worship today.

Temple at Belur,
photograph by Carol Guyer